FAVOURITE

CAKE

RECIPES

BOOK TWO

A Teatime Collection
compiled by Lucy Rose

illustrated by
Birket Foster RWS

SALMON

Index

Cover pictures *front:* "Winding the Wool"   *back:* "Feeding the Ducklings"
Title page: "Removing the Thorn"

Printed and Published by J. Salmon Ltd., Sevenoaks, England © Copyright

Caribbean Cake

A simple-to-make sponge loaf cake containing lime juice,
banana chips and desiccated coconut..

6 oz self raising flour   6 oz butter, softened   6 oz caster sugar
1½ oz desiccated coconut   1½ oz banana chips, finely crushed
Grated rind and juice of 1 lime   3 medium eggs

TOPPING
3-4 tablespoons icing sugar
Juice of ½ a lime   Desiccated coconut for sprinkling

Set oven to 350°F or Mark 4. Grease and line a 1 lb loaf tin. Put all the cake ingredients into a bowl and beat very well for about 2 minutes, using a wooden spoon. Put into the tin and bake for about 50 to 60 minutes until golden brown and firm and a skewer inserted comes out clean. Allow to cool in the tin before turning out on to a wire rack. When cold make the topping. Mix the icing sugar with just sufficient of the lime juice, spoon the icing over the cake and spread out. Sprinkle the top with desiccated coconut.

Although a number of the following recipes specify the use of butter, a satisfactory result can generally be obtained by using soft margarine. However, butter will give the cake a better flavour.

Chocolate Brownies

A nutty chocolate treat; a perennial favourite with all ages.

4 oz good plain chocolate	**1 teaspoon baking powder**
4 oz butter	**5 oz caster sugar**
2 oz flour	**3 eggs, beaten**

4 oz chopped mixed nuts

Set oven to 350°F or Mark 4. Grease and line an 8 inch square baking tin. Melt the chocolate and butter together in a bowl set over, but not touching, a pan of simmering water. Sift the flour and baking powder into a mixing bowl, add the sugar, pour over the chocolate mixture and mix well together. Stir in the eggs and chopped nuts and mix well. Put into the tin, spread out and bake for 25 to 30 minutes until a skewer inserted comes out clean. Leave to cool in the tin for 10 minutes, cut into squares and turn out on to a wire rack.

Honey Cake

A delicious, honey-flavoured plain cake. Blended honey works well.

8 oz honey	**8 oz self raising flour**
4 oz butter, softened	**Pinch of salt**
2 eggs, well beaten	**Milk, if necessary**
6 oz sultanas	

Set oven to 325°F or Mark 3. Grease and line a 6½ to 7 inch round cake tin. In a bowl, cream together the honey and butter then mix in the eggs alternately with the sifted flour and salt, reserving a little flour to add with the sultanas. Beat the mixture well but lightly, adding a little milk if necessary to produce a soft consistency. Coat the sultanas with all the remaining flour and stir in. Put into the tin and bake for 1¼ to 1½ hours until a skewer inserted comes out clean. Turn out on a wire rack to cool.

Banana Cake

This cake can be eaten plain or turned into a party cake, sandwiched with jam and whipped cream. It is easy to make in a food processor.

9 oz self raising flour	10 oz sugar
½ teaspoon bicarbonate soda	4 oz butter, softened
½ teaspoon salt	2 eggs
1 teaspoon vanilla essence	3-4 ripe bananas

Jam or whipped cream to sandwich, if preferred

Set oven to 375°F or Mark 5. Grease and bottom line two 9 inch sandwich tins. This cake is best made in a food processor. Put all the ingredients, except the bananas, into the mixer bowl and mix on medium speed until blended. Well mash the bananas and mix with the blended mixture. Divide between the two tins, smooth out and bake for 25 to 30 minutes until springy and a skewer inserted comes out clean. Turn out on to a wire rack to cool. When cold and if preferred, sandwich with jam and/or whipped cream.

Raspberry Gateau

A light, almond flavoured sponge lusciously filled with fresh raspberries and whipped cream. If preferred, tinned raspberries, well drained, can be used instead.

**3 eggs   4 oz caster sugar   ¾ teaspoon almond essence
3 oz flour   4 oz chopped almonds**

TOPPING
1 pint double cream   2 punnets fresh raspberries   8 oz chopped toasted almonds

Set oven to 325°F or Mark 3. Grease and line an 8 inch round cake tin. Break the eggs into a bowl set over, but not touching, a pan of hot water, add the caster sugar and whisk together until the mixture is pale, very thick and twice its original bulk; an electric whisk is easiest for this operation. Sieve the flour over the surface of the mixture, add the chopped almonds and fold in carefully with a metal spoon. Put into the tin and bake for 45 to 50 minutes until springy and a skewer inserted comes out clean. Turn out on to a wire rack to cool. When cold, split the cake into three layers. Whip the cream until thick and mix about one third of the cream with the raspberries, breaking them up slightly (reserve a few whole ones for decoration). Cover the bottom and middle layers of the cake with raspberry cream and assemble. Cover the top and sides of the cake with the remaining cream. Decorate the top with the reserved raspberries and press the toasted almonds into the side to cover.

'A Rest on the Cobbles'

Cornflour Cake

A very light, plain cake.

4 oz butter, softened   8 oz caster sugar
4 eggs, separated   Few drops of vanilla or almond essence
5 oz cornflour   9 oz flour   1 teaspoon baking powder   Pinch of salt
Icing sugar for sprinkling

Set oven to 375°F or Mark 5. Grease and line an 8 inch round cake tin. Cream together the butter and 4 oz of the sugar in a bowl until light and fluffy. Beat the egg yolks with the remaining 4 oz sugar until creamy, add to the butter mixture and beat thoroughly. Stir in the vanilla or almond essence. Sieve the cornflour, flour, baking powder and salt into the bowl and fold into the mixture. Whisk the egg whites until they stand in soft peaks and carefully fold in. Put into the tin and bake for 1 to $1\frac{1}{4}$ hours until a skewer inserted comes out clean. Cool in the tin for 5 minutes then turn out on to a wire rack. When cold, dust the top with sifted icing sugar.

Spicy Lemon Cake

A simple lemon cake flavoured with cinnamon and ginger and sandwiched with lemon curd. It improves with keeping for 48 hours before cutting.

6 oz butter, softened   6 oz caster sugar   2 large eggs, beaten
Pinch of salt   ½ teaspoon ground cinnamon   1 teaspoon ground ginger
8 oz self raising flour
Grated rind and juice of 1 large lemon
1 tablespoon milk   Lemon curd for filling

Set oven to 325°F or Mark 3. Grease and line a 7 inch round cake tin. Cream together the butter and sugar in a bowl until light and fluffy. Add the beaten eggs, salt, cinnamon and ginger, sieve in the flour and mix well. Finally, add the lemon rind and juice and the milk and mix all together. Put in the tin and bake for about 1 hour until firm and pale brown and a skewer inserted comes out clean. Leave to cool in the tin for 15 minutes then turn out on to a wire rack. When cold, split the cake in half and sandwich with lemon curd, preferably home made.

Poppy Seed Cake

A Madeira-type cake with the addition of crunchy poppy seeds.

4½ oz butter, softened	2 large eggs
4½ oz caster sugar	4½ oz self raising flour
½ teaspoon vanilla essence	1 oz poppy seeds
½ teaspoon orange essence	3 fl. oz milk

Orange marmalade to decorate

Set oven to 300°F or Mark 2. Grease and line a 6 inch round cake tin. Cream together the butter, sugar and essences in a bowl until light and fluffy. Beat in the eggs a little at a time with a little flour. Fold in the remaining flour with the poppy seeds, with sufficient of the milk to produce a soft consistency. Put into the tin and bake for 35 to 45 minutes until a skewer inserted comes out clean. Leave in the tin for a few minutes then turn out on to a wire rack to cool. When cold, paint the top of the cake with a coating of warmed orange marmalade.

Quick-mix Fruit Cake

A simple, all-in-one, spicy family fruit cake.

8 oz soft margarine	1 oz walnuts, coarsely chopped
8 oz soft brown sugar	12 oz self raising flour
4 eggs, beaten	½ teaspoon ground cinnamon
8 oz mixed dried fruit	½ teaspoon mixed spice

Set oven to 300°F or Mark 2. Grease and line an 8 to 9 inch round cake tin. Put all the ingredients together into a mixing bowl and beat well for 2 to 3 minutes until thoroughly mixed. Put into the tin, smooth the top and bake for about 1¾ hours until a skewer inserted comes out clean. Leave in the tin for about 10 minutes then turn out on to a wire rack to cool.

Marmalade Cake

A well flavoured home-made marmalade is best to use in this cake.

8 oz self raising flour	Grated rind of 1 orange
Pinch of salt	2 eggs, beaten
4 oz butter, softened	2 tablespoons orange marmalade
3 oz caster sugar	2 tablespoons milk
Few drops of vanilla essence	

7½" tin works OK

Set oven to 350°F or Mark 4. Grease and line a 6 inch round cake tin. Sift the flour and salt into a bowl and rub in the butter until the mixture resembles breadcrumbs. Stir in the sugar and 1 teaspoon of grated orange rind and then add the eggs, marmalade, milk and vanilla essence. Mix well together to the consistency of a thick batter. Spoon into the tin and bake for about 1 hour 20 minutes until golden and a skewer inserted comes out clean. Leave in the tin to cool for about 10 minutes before turning out on to a wire rack. Brush the top with a little warmed orange marmalade and sprinkle with the remaining orange rind.

Swiss Roll

A classic jam roll using a fat-less sponge mixture.

3 eggs   3 oz caster sugar   3 oz flour   Caster sugar for sprinkling
Raspberry jam, warmed   Icing sugar for sprinkling

Set oven to 325°F or Mark 3. Grease and line an approx 13 x 9 inches Swiss roll tin. Allow the greased baking paper to extend above the sides of the tin and cut the corners neatly to fit. Break the eggs into a bowl set over, but not touching, a pan of hot water, add the caster sugar and whisk together until the mixture is pale, very thick and twice its original bulk; an electric whisk is easiest for this operation. Sieve the flour over the surface of the mixture and fold in carefully with a metal spoon. Put into the tin, spread out evenly and bake for 8 to 10 minutes until golden brown. Meanwhile, wring out a thin teatowel in hot water and lay flat on the work surface. Cut a piece of baking paper larger than the cake tin, lay flat on the teatowel and sprinkle liberally with caster sugar. When cooked, turn the cake upside down on the sugared paper, remove the tin and carefully peel off the lining paper. Trim the long edges and spread a layer of warmed jam all over the surface of the cake. Make a score with a knife across the cake about ½ inch from the rolling edge to start the roll. Using the paper, carefully fold over from the scored short edge, make a firm first turn and then roll up neatly, pulling over the paper until the roll is completed. Leave *in situ* to cool. When cold, remove the paper and sprinkle with icing sugar.

Batley Cake

*This round cake is made on a baking sheet, not in a tin and has
a layer of jam through the middle. It comes from Yorkshire.*

**12 oz flour   3½ teaspoons baking powder   ½ teaspoon salt
6 oz butter, softened   6 oz caster sugar   1 egg, beaten   Milk to mix
2-3 dessertspoons apricot jam (or to choice)
Beaten egg to glaze**

Set oven to 350°F or Mark 4. Grease and flour a baking sheet. Sift the flour, baking powder and salt into a bowl and rub in the butter until the mixture resembles breadcrumbs. Mix in the sugar, add the beaten egg and mix to a stiff consistency with only a very little milk, if necessary. Divide the mixture in half and roll out two rounds about ½ inch thick on a lightly floured surface. If the jam is stiff, warm slightly in a bowl over hot water to facilitate spreading. Spread one round with a good layer of jam, cover with the other and pinch the edges together. Brush the top with beaten egg, place on the baking sheet and bake for 30 to 35 minutes until golden and a skewer inserted comes out clean. Transfer to a wire rack to cool.

Date Slices

*A shortbread mixture made with the addition of porridge oats
and filled with softened dates – a slice for a sweet tooth.*

8 oz stoned dates	1 teaspoon bicarbonate of soda
5 fl. oz water	4 oz butter, softened
½ teaspoon almond essence	4 oz quick porridge oats
4 oz self raising flour	6 oz caster sugar

Icing sugar for sprinkling

Set oven to 350°F or Mark 4. Grease and bottom line an approx. 7 x 11 inch baking tin. Chop the dates, put into a pan with the water, bring to the boil and cook gently until soft. Remove from the heat, stir in the essence and allow to cool. Sift the flour and bicarbonate of soda into a bowl and rub in the butter with the hands to form a soft dough. Rub in the oats and sugar and mix well together. Put half the mixture into the tin, spread out and press down firmly. Cover with the dates in an even layer, then top with the rest of the mixture and again press down firmly. Bake for 20 to 30 minutes until golden. Mark out into slices and leave in the tin to cool. When cold, sprinkle the top with icing sugar, cut into slices and turn out.

Apple and Hazlenut Cake

Apple cakes are always popular. This one includes hazelnuts with the raisins.

8 oz Bramley apples, weighed after peeling and coring
3 oz butter, softened   4 oz soft brown sugar
2 eggs   8 oz flour   1 teaspoon baking powder
½ teaspoon bicarbonate of soda   ½ teaspoon ground cinnamon
2 oz raisins   2 oz chopped hazelnuts

Set oven to 325°F or Mark 3. Grease and line a 2 lb loaf tin. First, peel, core and slice the apples and cook in a pan with just a very little water, until reduced to a pulp. Cream together the butter and sugar in a bowl until light and fluffy. Beat in the eggs one at a time with a little flour. Sift in the remaining flour with the baking powder, bicarbonate of soda and cinnamon, add the apple purée, raisins and chopped nuts and mix well together. Put into the tin and bake for 70 to 80 minutes until a skewer inserted comes out clean. Leave in the tin for about 10 minutes then turn out on to a wire rack to cool.

Porter Cake

Porter was a dark brown ale, once widely used for cooking as well as drinking;
nowadays Guinness is used instead.

4 oz butter	1 teaspoon mixed spice
4 oz soft brown sugar	¼ pint Guinness
2 eggs, lightly beaten	6 oz raisins
8 oz flour	6 oz sultanas
½ teaspoon baking powder	Finely grated rind of 1 lemon

Set oven to 325°F or Mark 3. Grease and line a 7 inch round cake tin. Cream together the butter and sugar in a bowl until light and fluffy. Beat in the eggs, a little at a time with a little flour. Sift together the remaining flour, the baking powder and spice and fold into the mixture. Add the Guinness, beating well, then stir in the dried fruit and lemon rind. Put into the tin and bake for about 1½ hours until a skewer inserted comes out clean. Allow to cool completely in the tin, then wrap in greaseproof paper and kitchen foil and store for a week to 10 days before eating.

If desired, this cake can be fed halfway through storing time. Unwrap the cake, pierce a few holes in its base with a fine skewer and pour over a dessertspoon of Guinness. Leave for 40 minutes before rewrapping.

Rich Chocolate Cake

A fudge-type cake coated with apricot jam and chocolate icing, for special occasions.
It may sink and crack in cooling, but the icing will cover.

6 oz good plain chocolate   4 oz butter, softened   4 oz caster sugar
7 oz ground almonds   4 eggs, separated   5 tablespoons apricot jam

ICING
3 oz good plain chocolate   2 oz butter

Set oven to 350°F or Mark 4. Grease and line an 8 to 9 inch springform cake tin. Break up the chocolate and put into a bowl set over a pan of simmering water and stir until melted; remove from the heat. Cream together the butter and sugar in a bowl until light and fluffy. Stir in the ground almonds, egg yolks and melted chocolate and beat well together. Whisk the egg whites in a bowl until stiff and carefully fold into the mixture. Put into the tin and bake for 50 to 55 minutes until a skewer inserted comes out clean. Leave for a few minutes to cool then turn out on to a wire rack. When cold, coat the top with apricot jam, warmed if necessary. For the icing, cut 2 oz butter in pieces and put with 3 oz chocolate, broken up, in a bowl over a pan of simmering water. When melted, stir together and spread over the top of the cake, allowing the mixture to run down the sides.

Genoese Sponge Cake

A delicious and very light sponge cake sandwiched with jam and whipped cream.

3 eggs	2 oz melted butter
3 oz caster sugar	Raspberry jam (or to choice)
3 oz flour	5 fl.oz double cream

Icing sugar for sprinkling

Set oven to 325°F or Mark 3. Grease and dust with flour and caster sugar two 7 to 8 inch sandwich tins. Break the eggs into a bowl set over, but not touching, a pan of hot water, add the caster sugar and whisk together until the mixture is pale, very thick and twice its original bulk; an electric whisk is easiest for this operation. Sieve the flour over the surface of the mixture and fold in carefully with a metal spoon. Melt the butter in a pan, allow to cool slightly, then pour slowly down the side of the mixing bowl, folding in quickly and lightly. Divide between the two tins, smooth out and bake for 20 to 25 minutes until golden brown. Turn out on to a wire rack to cool. When cold, whip the cream to hold its peaks and sandwich the cakes with a layer of jam covered with a good layer of whipped cream. Sprinkle the top of the cake with icing sugar.

'Blackberrying'

Canadian Gingerbread

A traditional gingerbread made with black treacle and golden syrup.
This cake improves in flavour if it is kept for 48 hours.

10 oz flour	**4 oz soft brown sugar**
1 teaspoon bicarbonate of soda	**6 oz black treacle**
2 teaspoons ground ginger	**6 oz golden syrup**
2 teaspoons ground cinnamon	**2 eggs, beaten**
4 oz butter	**¼ pint boiling water**

Set oven to 350°F or Mark 4. Grease and line an approx. 8 inch square deep cake tin. Sift the flour, bicarbonate of soda and spices into a large bowl. Melt the butter, sugar, black treacle and golden syrup in a pan over a gentle heat then pour into the dry ingredients. Mix well. Stir in the beaten eggs and, lastly, add the boiling water and mix. Pour into the tin and bake for 40 to 45 minutes until firm and a skewer inserted comes out clean. Turn out on to a wire rack to cool.

Nussküchen

*A coffee and hazelnut sponge cake sandwiched with
a succulent apple and apricot jam filling.*

**4 oz butter, softened   4 oz caster sugar   2 eggs, separated
1½ oz ground roasted hazelnuts   4 oz self raising flour   Pinch of salt
1 teaspoon instant coffee granules   1 tablespoon warm milk**

FILLING
**1 lb dessert apples, peeled, cored and sliced   Grated rind and juice of ½ a lemon
2 tablespoons apricot jam   Icing sugar for sprinkling**

Set oven to 375°F or Mark 5. Grease and line an 8 inch round cake tin. Roast
the nuts in the oven, rub off the skins and grind. Cream together the butter and
sugar in a bowl until light and fluffy. Add the egg yolks, nuts, flour and salt
and mix well. Dissolve the coffee granules in the warm milk, add to the
mixture and mix in. Beat the egg whites stiffly and carefully fold into the
mixture. Put into the tin and bake for about 45 minutes until firm and a skewer
inserted comes out clean. Turn out on to a wire rack to cool. Meanwhile,
make the filling. Put the apple slices, lemon rind and juice and the jam in a
pan, cover and cook gently until soft. Allow to cool. When cold, split the cake
in half and fill with the apple mixture. To finish, sprinkle the top of the cake
with icing sugar.

Pineapple and Brazil Nut Cake

A light, moist, nutty cake flavoured with pineapple.

7 oz butter, softened
5 oz caster sugar
3 eggs, beaten
9 oz self raising flour

½ a 430gm tin crushed pineapple
6 oz shelled Brazil nuts, chopped
1 tablespoon water
2 tablespoons Demerara sugar

Pineapple glacé icing

Set oven to 325°F or Mark 3. Grease and line a 7 inch round cake tin. Cream together the butter and sugar in a bowl until light and fluffy. Beat in the eggs with a little flour, then fold in the remaining flour. Stir in the pineapple with its juice followed by 4 oz of the chopped nuts and the water. Put into the tin, smooth the top and sprinkle with the Demerara sugar. Bake for about 1¼ hours until a skewer inserted comes out clean. Leave in the tin for 10 minutes and then turn out on to a wire rack to cool. When cold, cover the top with glacé icing and sprinkle with the remaining chopped nuts. To make the icing, take about 4 oz icing sugar and mix with it just sufficient crushed pineapple to produce a stiff spreading consistency.

Penzance Cake

This easy-to-make craggy fruit cake looks rather like a great big rock cake.
It is best kept for a day before cutting.

1 lb self raising flour	**2 oz chopped mixed peel**
Pinch of salt	**3 oz stem ginger, finely chopped**
2 teaspoons ground cinnamon	**3 large eggs, beaten**
4 oz butter, softened	**3 fl.oz clear honey, warmed**
1 lb currants	**3 fl.oz milk, warmed**

Set oven to 350°F or Mark 4. Grease and line an 8 inch round cake tin. Sift the flour, salt and cinnamon together into a bowl and rub in the butter until the mixture resembles breadcrumbs. Stir in the currants, mixed peel and stem ginger. Warm the honey and milk together. Add the beaten eggs to the bowl and then mix in with sufficient of the honey/milk mixture to produce a soft but not sticky dough. Put into the tin and bake for 1 to $1\frac{1}{2}$ hours until a skewer inserted comes out clean. Leave to cool in the tin.

Coffee Walnut Cake

A delicious, moist and easy-to-make cake – a perennial favourite at coffee mornings and tea parties.

6 oz self raising flour   6 oz caster sugar   6 oz soft margarine
3 eggs, beaten   2 teaspoons instant coffee granules

FILLING AND TOPPING
8 oz icing sugar   4 oz butter, softened
1 tablespoon coffee essence   Walnut halves to decorate

Set oven to 325°F or Mark 3. Grease and bottom line two 7 inch sandwich tins. Put the flour, sugar and margarine into a mixing bowl. Beat the eggs in a bowl, add the coffee granules and mix until dissolved. Then add the eggs to the dry ingredients, stir together and beat well for 2 minutes or until well blended. Divide between the tins, spread out and bake for about 20 minutes until golden brown, springy to the touch and a skewer inserted comes out clean. Turn out on to a wire rack to cool. Make the filling by blending together the icing sugar, butter and coffee essence and use to sandwich the cakes and ice the top. To finish, decorate with walnut halves.

Angel Cake

An American party cake which has a light, fine texture and is coated with glacé icing.

6 large egg whites   ½ teaspoon cream of tartar
6 oz caster sugar   Few drops of vanilla essence
4 oz flour   Glacé icing
Glacé cherries and angelica pieces to decorate

Set oven to 300°F or Mark 2. Grease and flour an 8 to 9 inch ring tin. Whisk the egg whites in a bowl until very stiff; an electric whisk is easiest for this operation. Carefully fold in the sugar. Sift the flour with the cream of tartar into the bowl and fold in and, finally, fold in the vanilla essence. Put into the ring tin, spread out evenly and bake for about 1 hour until shrunk back from the side and a skewer inserted comes out clean. Invert the tin over a wire rack and leave to get cold, when the cake should drop out. When cold, ice all over with glacé icing and decorate with glacé cherries and angelica pieces. To make the icing, dissolve 8 oz icing sugar with just enough warm water to produce a spreadable consistency.

Chocolate and Apple Cake

Sandwiched and topped with a thick layer of chocolate butter icing, this is a rich cake made extra moist with the addition of chopped apples.

**9 oz flour   1 oz cocoa powder   1 teaspoon baking powder
1 teaspoon bicarbonate of soda   4 oz butter, softened   9 oz caster sugar
2 eggs   Few drops of vanilla essence   6 fl.oz milk
2 medium cooking apples, peeled, cored and finely chopped**

ICING

180c

1 lb icing sugar   1 oz cocoa powder   2 oz butter, softened   3 fl.oz milk

Set oven to 350°F or Mark 4. Grease and line a 7 to 8 inch round cake tin. Sieve together into a bowl the flour, cocoa powder, baking powder and bicarbonate of soda and set aside. Cream together the butter and sugar in a bowl and whisk with an electric whisk until light and fluffy. Whisk in the eggs one at a time and add the vanilla essence. Then whisk in the flour with the milk, a little at a time. Finally mix in the finely chopped apples. Put into the tin and bake for 50 to 60 minutes until a skewer inserted comes out clean. Leave in the tin for 10 minutes then turn out on to a wire rack to cool. When cold, split the cake in half, sandwich with a good layer of butter icing and spread the remaining icing over the top. To make the icing, put all the ingredients into a bowl and beat with an electric whisk on slow speed until creamy.

Thirty-Four

Whisky Cake

A Scotch whisky flavoured sponge cake, sandwiched and coated
with honey and orange butter icing.

6 oz butter   6 oz soft brown sugar   Grated rind of 1 small orange
3 eggs, beaten   6 oz self-raising flour   4 tablespoons whisky

ICING
6 oz icing sugar   2 oz butter, softened
2 tablespoons clear honey   1 tablespoon orange juice
Toasted flaked almonds to decorate

Set oven to 375°F or Mark 5. Grease and bottom line two 7 inch sandwich tins. Cream together the butter and sugar in a bowl. Add the orange rind. Beat in the eggs one at a time and whisk until the mixture is pale and fluffy. Sift in about half the flour, add the whisky and fold into the mixture. Sift in the remaining flour and fold in. Divide between the two tins and smooth over. Bake for 20 to 25 minutes until light golden and a skewer inserted comes out clean. Turn out on to a wire rack to cool. To make the icing, put the butter into a bowl, add the honey and orange juice, sift in the icing sugar slowly and work the mixture gradually until the ingredients are combined. Sandwich the cakes together with half of the buttercream. Use the remainder to cover the top of the cake and decorate with toasted almonds.

Carrot and Fruit Cake

A delicious variety of carrot cake, made with wholemeal flour and with honey, sultanas and orange juice.

4 oz unsalted butter, softened
2 oz soft brown sugar
2 oz clear honey
3 large eggs, beaten
8 oz wholemeal flour

2 teaspoons baking powder
6 oz carrots, finely grated
3 oz sultanas
3 oz ground almonds
Grated rind and juice of 1 orange

150 C

Set oven to 300°F or Mark 2. Grease and line a 7 inch round cake tin. Cream together the butter, sugar and honey in a bowl until light and fluffy. Gradually beat in the eggs, adding a little flour towards the end. Fold in the remaining flour with the baking powder and mix in the grated carrot, sultanas and ground almonds. Finally, fold in the grated orange rind and juice. Put into the tin and bake for $1\frac{1}{2}$ to 2 hours until a skewer inserted comes out clean. Leave in the tin for a few minutes then turn out on to a wire rack to cool.

Fresh Cherry Cake

A superb summer cake made with fresh cherries which give it a delightful flavour.

9 oz self raising flour	**2 large eggs, beaten**
5 oz butter, softened	**4 fl.oz milk**
5 oz ground almonds	**10 oz fresh dessert cherries, stoned**
5 oz caster sugar	**1 oz flaked almonds**

Set oven to 350°F or Mark 4. Grease and line an 8 inch round cake tin. Sieve the flour into a mixing bowl and rub in the butter until the mixture resembles breadcrumbs. Stir in the ground almonds and sugar, then add the eggs, milk and cherries. Mix carefully until combined, but do not over mix. Spoon into the tin and smooth over. Scatter the flaked almonds over the top and bake for about 1 hour 10 minutes until the cake is golden and firm to the touch and a skewer inserted comes out clean. Leave to cool in the tin for 10 minutes then turn out on to a wire rack.

Paradise Cake

Cherry, walnut and almond slices filled with apricot jam.

8 oz shortcrust pastry
Apricot jam
4 oz butter, softened
4 oz caster sugar
2 small eggs, beaten
2 tablespoons chopped glacé cherries

2 tablespoons chopped walnuts
2 oz ground almonds
2 oz ground rice
1 oz self raising flour
½ teaspoon almond essence
Caster sugar for sprinkling

Set oven to 350°F or Mark 4. Grease and bottom line an approx 7 x 11 inches baking tin. Roll out the pastry on a lightly floured surface and use to line the base of the tin. Spread a layer of apricot jam over the pastry. Cream together the butter and sugar in a bowl until light and fluffy then beat in the eggs, a little at a time. Add all the rest of the ingredients to the bowl and stir well together. Spread the mixture over the jam and smooth out. Bake for 30 to 40 minutes until golden brown. As soon as the tin is out of the oven, sprinkle with caster sugar. Leave to cool in the tin then turn out on to a wire rack. When cold, cut into fingers.

Black Forest Gateau

This is a simple version of an old favourite.

8 oz butter   8 oz caster sugar   4 eggs, beaten
2 tablespoons cocoa powder   A little water to mix
8 oz self raising flour   450gm tin black cherries
1 teaspoon arrowroot   2-3 teaspoons Kirsch   1½ pints double cream
3 oz grated chocolate for decorating

Set oven to 325°F or Mark 3. Grease and base line two 8 inch sandwich tins. Cream together the butter and sugar in a bowl until light and fluffy. Gradually beat in the eggs with a little flour. Blend the cocoa powder with a little water to form a paste, mix in, alternately, with the remaining flour and combine well together. Divide between the tins and bake for about 30 minutes until springy to the touch and a skewer inserted comes out clean. Turn out on to a wire rack to cool. When cold, split each cake in half. Drain the cherries and reserve the juice. Blend the arrowroot with the juice, boil to thicken, stirring, then add the Kirsch. Allow to cool. Whip the cream until thick. Spread cream on each cake layer, except the top, cover with halved cherries (reserving some whole cherries for decoration) and spread over them the thickened juice. Assemble the cake, cover the plain top and sides with cream, decorate with reserved cherries on top and sprinkle grated chocolate around the sides.

Sugar-free Fruit Cake

This cake has no added sugar; the sweetness comes from the dried fruit and honey.

12 oz flour	2¾ oz glacé cherries, halved
2 teaspoons baking powder	3½ oz raisins
1 teaspoon mixed spice	4 fl. oz milk
4½ oz butter, softened	2 eggs, beaten
2¾ oz 'no-soak' apricots, chopped	Grated rind of 1 orange
2¾ oz dates, stoned and chopped	5-6 teaspoons orange juice

3 tablespoons clear honey

Set oven to 350°F or Mark 4. Grease and line an 8 inch round cake tin. Sieve the flour, baking powder and spice into a bowl and rub in the butter until the mixture resembles breadcrumbs. Stir in all the dried fruit, milk, eggs and orange rind and juice then mix in the honey to produce a soft dropping consistency. Put into the tin and bake for 1 to 1½ hours until a skewer inserted comes out clean. Turn out on to a wire rack to cool.

Mothering Sunday Cake

This variation of Simnel Cake resembles a rich, curranty loaf rather than the more usual marzipan-decorated Easter cake.

8 oz self raising flour	4 oz currants
1½ oz butter, softened	4 oz sultanas
1½ oz lard	2 oz chopped candied peel
5 oz caster sugar	2 oz ground almonds
½ teaspoon ground cinnamon	1 large egg
½ teaspoon ground nutmeg	Milk to mix

Set oven to 350°F or Mark 4. Grease and flour a baking sheet. Sift the flour into a bowl and rub in the fats until the mixture resembles breadcrumbs. Add the sugar, spices, dried fruit, peel and ground almonds and mix well. Break the egg into a bowl, combine very lightly with a fork – do not beat – and stir into the mixture with a little milk, if necessary, to produce a *very stiff* dough. As the cake is not confined in a tin, the dough *must* be stiff enough to hold its shape during cooking. Form the dough into a round on a floured surface, put on the baking sheet and brush with milk to glaze. Bake for about 40 to 50 minutes until a skewer inserted comes out clean. Be prepared for the cake to 'spread' a little. Cool on a wire rack.

Ginger Sponge Squares

A delicious combination of ginger flavoured sponge and lemon icing.

3 oz butter	Pinch of salt
2 oz Demerara sugar	2 teaspoons ground ginger
8 oz golden syrup	1 large egg
8 oz self raising flour	2½ fl oz milk
Lemon glacé icing	Crystallised ginger to decorate

Set oven to 325°F or Mark 3. Grease and bottom line an approx. 8 inch square baking tin. Melt together the butter, sugar and golden syrup in a pan over a gentle heat but do not allow to get too hot. Sift the flour, salt and ground ginger into a bowl and stir in the syrup mixture. Break the egg into the milk, beat together, add to the mixture and stir well. Pour into the tin, spread out and bake for about 45 minutes until a skewer inserted comes out clean. Turn out on to a wire rack to cool. When cold, ice with lemon glacé icing, cut into squares and decorate each square with a piece of crystallised ginger.

Christmas Cake

The variations of Christmas cake are legion and most families have their favourite.
For an extra moist cake, make 4 to 6 weeks in advance and pierce and feed
with brandy or rum each week.

6 oz butter, softened   6 oz soft brown sugar   1 tablespoon black treacle
4 eggs, beaten   8 oz flour   2 teaspoons mixed spice
1 lb mixed dried fruit   2 oz blanched almonds, chopped
4 oz chopped mixed peel   2 oz glacé cherries, chopped
2 teaspoons grated lemon rind   1 tablespoon brandy or dark rum

Set oven to 325°F or Mark 3. Grease and line an 8 to 8½ inch round cake tin with a double layer of greaseproof paper. Wrap a double layer of brown paper around the tin and secure with string. Cream together the butter, sugar and treacle in a bowl until pale and fluffy. Gradually add the eggs, beating each addition thoroughly. Sift in the flour with the mixed spice and stir in, mixing well. Add the dried fruit, almonds, peel, cherries, lemon rind and brandy or rum and mix to a dropping consistency, adding a little milk if necessary. Put into the tin, make a hollow in the top and bake for 30 minutes then reduce oven to 300°F or Mark 2 and continue for a further 3 to 3½ hours until the cake has shrunk slightly from the tin and a skewer inserted comes out clean. Leave to cool in the tin. Eat plain or decorate with marzipan and frosted icing.

Lemon and Poppy Seed Cake

An Australian ring sponge cake flavoured with lemon and poppy seeds
and finished with a soft lemon glacé icing.

1 oz poppy seeds   4 fl.oz warm milk   8 oz self raising flour
6 oz butter, softened   8 oz caster sugar
3 eggs   Grated rind of 2 lemons

ICING
8 oz icing sugar   1 oz butter, softened   Lemon juice

Set oven to 325°F or Mark 3. Grease and flour an 8 to 9 inch ring tin. First, soak the poppy seeds in the warm milk for 10 to 15 minutes. When ready, put all the ingredients, including the poppy seed milk, into a bowl and beat well together for about 2 minutes. Put into the tin, spread out and bake for about 45 minutes until golden brown and a skewer inserted comes out clean. Leave to cool in the tin for a few minutes then turn out on to a wire rack. When cold, ice with lemon butter icing. To make the icing, cream together the sugar and butter and mix in just sufficient lemon juice to produce a spreading consistency.

METRIC CONVERSIONS

The weights, measures and oven temperatures used in the preceding recipes can be easily converted to their metric equivalents. The conversions listed below are only approximate, having been rounded up or down as may be appropriate.

Weights

Avoirdupois	Metric
1 oz.	just under 30 grams
4 oz. (¼ lb.)	app. 115 grams
8 oz. (½ lb.)	app. 230 grams
1 lb.	454 grams

Liquid Measures

Imperial	Metric
1 tablespoon (liquid only)	20 millilitres
1 fl. oz.	app. 30 millilitres
1 gill (¼ pt.)	app. 145 millilitres
½ pt.	app. 285 millilitres
1 pt.	app. 570 millilitres
1 qt.	app. 1.140 litres

Oven Temperatures

	°Fahrenheit	Gas Mark	°Celsius
Slow	300	2	150
	325	3	170
Moderate	350	4	180
	375	5	190
	400	6	200
Hot	425	7	220
	450	8	230
	475	9	240

Flour as specified in these recipes refers to plain flour unless otherwise descri'